super-duper cupcakes

kids' creations from the Cupcake Caboose

super-duper cupcakes

kids' creations from the Cupcake Caboose

ELAINE COHEN

Sterling Publishing Co., Inc.
New York

Library of Congress Cataloging-in-Publication Data

10 9 8 7 6 5 4 3

Cohen, Elaine.
  Super-duper cupcakes : kids creations from the cupcake caboose / Elaine Cohen.
    p. cm.
  ISBN-13: 978-1-4027-2174-8
  ISBN-10: 1-4027-2174-9
  1. Cake decorating--Juvenile literature. 2. Cake--Juvenile literature. I. Title.

TX771.2.C64 2006
641.8'6539--dc22

               2005032097

Designed by Barbara Scott-Goodman
Photos by Zeva Oelbaum
Illustrations by Vic Kulihian

Published by Sterling Publishing Co., Inc.
387 Park Avenue South, New York, NY 10016
© 2006 by Elaine Cohen
www.cupcakecaboose.com
Distributed in Canada by Sterling Publishing
c/o Canadian Manda Group, 165 Dufferin Street
Toronto, Ontario, Canada M6K 3H6
Distributed in the United Kingdom by GMC Distribution Services
Castle Place, 166 High Street, Lewes, East Sussex, England BN71XU
Distributed in Australia by Capricorn Link (Australia) Pty. Ltd.,
P.O. Box 704, Windsor, NSW 2756, Australia

Printed in China
All rights reserved

Sterling ISBN-13: 978-1-4027-2174-8
       ISBN-10: 1-4027-2174-9

For information about custom editions, special sales, premium and
corporate purchases, please contact Sterling Special Sales
Department at 800-805-5489 or specialsales@sterlingpub.com.

acknowledgments

I'm incredibly lucky to have been able to write this book. And I'm equally, if not more, lucky to have such wonderful people in my life.

If it weren't for Danielle Truscott's faith and encouragement, I never would have been involved in this project. Heather Quinlan, my editor, with the assistance of Becky Maines, offered clear and insightful direction all the way through. Nina Ong, Wendy Palitz, and Barbara Scott-Goodman paved the way for a great design. Zeva Oelbaum, Effie Paroutsas, and Sara Neumeier were masterful in creating wonderfully styled photos. Thank you for making a dream come to life.

My loving and loyal friends have given immense amounts of support. They remind me to live my most creative and meaningful life: Jane Dowling, Shayna Samuels, Alison Goldberg, Batyah Sthrum, Erica Karsch, Elke Katz, Josiana Bianchi, Christine McQuade, Jennie Komittee, Nina Ong, Sarah Maltby, and Zelina Blagden. Additionally, I thank Dillon Jaime Paul, my dearest of friends, who inspired the delicious cupcake adventure. I'm so fortunate to have all of you in my life.

I greatly appreciate the generosity and love given to me by Debbie Allee, Dennis Mincielli, Mike Mincielli, John S. Allee, Johnny, Jena, Jack, and Will Allee. Thank you for being part of my family.

I'm deeply grateful for my mom, Caron Lee Cohen, for her unconditional love and limitless exuberance for life. Thank you for all the fun we've had in and out of the kitchen, for explaining the importance of nature, and for all the guidance in writing this book and living my life. You are my sunshine.

My life would only be semisweet if it weren't for David Sellier Allee. Hands down, he's the most adorable cupcake in the world and certainly my most ideal partner in life. I'm thankful every morning that I can wake up to see his beautiful mug.

Lastly, I thank my dad, William Henry Cohen, whom I miss terribly. On most days, though, I feel the warmth of his hand and hear his sweet words of affection. I loved our thirty-one years together immensely.

Table of Contents

Welcome!

Let's spend an afternoon in the kitchen crafting cupcakes with color and candy.

You can create beautiful butterflies, Thanksgiving pumpkins, slithering snakes, and many other decorations on your very own little cakes. And after I show you some ideas, you can go on and decorate in many other ways that are special to you. Whatever your favorite things in the world are, you can add them to a cupcake.

All the designs in this book can be made with easy-to-find items. Whether you make the cupcakes and frosting homemade, get a cake mix, or buy packaged items, you will have great fun in putting together these treats.

Your local supermarket has many of the items you will need to get started. Other equipment can be found around the house and in the kitchen. A few ingredients can be collected in specialty shops.

Okay, it's time to start "cupcaking."

Collect the foods and tools

Tools are necessary for any job. It's actually part of the fun to collect the bits and pieces you need to get started. So, gather the foods—cupcakes, frosting, candy—and the kitchen supplies listed in the next few pages. And then you can begin.

why are they called cupcakes?

They get their name from the little paper wrapper and the individual-portion pans that the cake batter is baked in. They are also called cupcakes because of the amount of ingredients used to bake them—a cupful of this, a cupful of that.

What could be more special than having your own individual mini cake? It's your dessert and yours alone.

Let's go!

So, the cupcakes for our cupcaking activities can be baked at home, made from a mix, or bought already prepared.

Homemade

These are the ingredients you will need. It's best to use the freshest foods for baking (and cooking too!):
eggs, butter, milk, flour, sugar, vanilla extract, cocoa, baking soda, baking powder, salt, water, applesauce.

Recipes for Deep Dark Chocolate Cupcakes and Vanilla Heaven Cupcakes can be found on pages 20 and 22.

Cake Mix

This is fairly easy, and fun. All you have to do is collect the few foods listed on the back of the box and then follow the directions. You will need: cake mix, eggs, oil or butter, applesauce, water.

Pre-made

You are all set to go!
Try to find pre-packaged cupcakes that are big, so there is plenty of space to decorate. If you like, you can trim the frosting edges to make a clean line around the top of the cupcake or even peel off the chocolate frosting.
It's up to you.

Health-Conscious Recipe

Cake mix boxes often list a health-conscious recipe, which typically includes applesauce. I find this to be a good option, so try it.

Frosting

Ah, the frosting . . . some say frosting is the best part of any cake. Which do you like better, the cake or the frosting? Well, the frosting you use for cupcaking can be made at home, prepared from a mix, or bought already made. In my opinion, there is a huge difference between homemade frosting and packaged frosting. I like the homemade kind a lot more! Recipes for coloring frosting are on page 15.

Homemade

Here are the ingredients you need to make some:
butter, confectioners' sugar, vanilla extract, milk, heavy cream, cocoa, salt.
Hands down—the taste of buttercream frosting is best when it's made with organic butter. It tastes creamier and more luscious.

Delicious Vanilla Buttercream Frosting and Chocolate Buttercream Frosting recipes can be found on page 24.

Frosting Mix

Follow the directions on the box.

Packaged

Choose a packaged frosting that has a flavor you like. Whipped frostings are often the easiest to spread.

What's Organic?

Foods that are made or grown without chemicals.

Color your frosting

Experimenting with food coloring and frosting is loads of fun. It's like painting. The food coloring sold at most grocery stores is fine and works well. But if there is a specialty cake supply store in your neighborhood, peek in and check out the array of concentrated color pastes you can buy. They are amazing.

Another alternative is vegetable- or fruit-based food colorings. Try making a red color by mashing strawberries or raspberries in a bowl and then pouring the liquid through a strainer. To make a blue color, you can crush blueberries. These are worth trying, but may have strong flavors.

The most important thing to remember is to add a very small amount of food coloring to your frosting at first. Then you can add more food coloring to create a brighter color.

color tints

To Make Pink: *1 little drop of red food coloring*

To Make Red: *2 drops of red food coloring*

To Make Orange: *1 little drop of red plus 1 little drop of yellow food coloring*

To Make Yellow: *2 drops of yellow food coloring*

To Make Green: *2 drops of green food coloring*

To Make Blue: *2 drops of blue food coloring*

To Make Gray: *1 drop of blue, 1 drop of red, and 1 drop of green food coloring*

To Make Purple: *1 drop of blue and 1 drop of red food coloring*

To Make Brown: *2 drops each of blue, red, yellow, and green food coloring*

Decorations

Listed below are the candies you need to create the decorations in this book. You have a rainbow of colors and many shapes and sizes to play with. What fun!

Candy dots

Licorice string

Chocolate sprinkles

Tiny, oval-shaped hard candies

Tiny, fruit-flavored jelly candies

Candy orange slices

Fruit gem candies

Sour cherries

Green apple strip candy

Marzipan

Nonpareils

Chocolate

Decorating gels

Brightly colored disk-shaped candies

Swedish fish

Fruit-shaped candies

Little candy-coated gums

Colored sugar decorations

Mini marshmallows

Mexican hats

Mini candy-coated chocolates

Licorice

Equipment

You may already have in your kitchen many of the gizmos and gadgets listed on this page. If not, a local market or household store will. Oh, and you could always ask a neighbor to lend you an item.

Muffin Pans

Baking Cup Liners

Bowls

Spoons

Knives

Fork

Whisk

Plates and Platters

Pastry Cutter

Electric Mixer

Measuring Cups

Scissors

Plastic Kitchen Bags

Waxed Paper

Tinfoil

Rubber Spatula

Wire Cooking Racks

Pencil

Toothpick

Baking Pan

Cookie Cutters

kitchen safety

Please remember this: You should ALWAYS have an adult help you when you are using an oven, a stove, or an electric mixer. Also, be careful using knives so that all of your time in the kitchen is fun and filled with smiles.

Recipes

Let's get busy in the kitchen. Do you like chocolate or vanilla cake? You pick. There's just something extra special about a cake made from scratch because YOU made it. Bravo!

deep dark chocolate cupcakes

You need:

½ cup cocoa, measured by spoon-and-sweep

1 cup very hot water

2 teaspoons pure vanilla extract

1¼ cups all-purpose flour, measured by dip-and-sweep

½ teaspoon baking soda

½ teaspoon salt

12 tablespoons (1½ sticks) unsalted butter, softened

1¼ cups sugar

2 large eggs, at room temperature

Makes about 12 cupcakes

Instructions:

1. Adjust the oven rack to the center position and preheat the oven to 350 degrees. Line muffin pans with bake cup liners.

2. Put the cocoa in a small bowl; add the hot water and mix until smooth. Cool to room temperature, and then stir in the vanilla extract.

3. Whisk together the flour, baking soda, and salt in a medium bowl.

Directions for Electric Mixer

4. Beat the butter with the mixer set at medium-high speed until smooth and shiny, about 15 seconds. Add the sugar; beat until the mixture is fluffy, about 2 minutes. Add the eggs and beat until fully incorporated, about 30 seconds.

5. With the mixer on the lowest speed, add about ⅓ of the dry ingredients to the batter, followed immediately by about ⅓ of the cocoa mixture; mix until the ingredients are almost incorporated into the batter. Repeat the process twice more. When the batter appears blended, stop the mixer and scrape the bowl sides with a rubber spatula. Return the mixer to low speed; beat until the batter looks satiny, about 15 seconds longer.

Directions for Hand Mix

4. Beat the butter with a large spoon until smooth and shiny, 2 to 3 minutes. Add the sugar; beat until the mixture is fluffy, 3 to 4 minutes. Add the eggs and beat until fully incorporated, about 1 minute.

5. Add ⅓ of the dry ingredients to the batter, and mix for 1 to 2 minutes. Add ⅓ of the cocoa mixture and mix until the ingredients are almost incorporated into batter, 1 to 2 minutes. Repeat the process twice more. When the batter appears blended, scrape the bowl sides with a rubber spatula. Mix for another minute, or until the batter looks satiny.

6. Pour the batter into muffin cups so that the cups are about 80% full. Bake the cupcakes for 17 to 20 minutes. Insert a toothpick into the center of a cupcake; if it comes out clean or with just a crumb adhering, it is done.

7. Transfer the muffin pans to wire cooling racks or away from the hot oven. Let them cool for 10 minutes. Place the cupcakes onto a rack or a plate so that they continue to cool. Be sure to cool the cupcakes completely before frosting, about 1 hour.

Baking Tip

When placing your muffin pans in the oven, arrange them at least 3 inches from the oven walls and 3 inches apart. If your oven is small, you should place the pans on separate racks in a staggered fashion to allow for air circulation.

vanilla heaven cupcakes

You need:

1 cup milk, at room temperature

¾ cup egg whites (about 6 large or 5 extra-large), at room temperature

1 teaspoon pure vanilla extract

2¼ cups plain cake flour (regular all-purpose flour can be substituted)

1¾ cup sugar

4 teaspoons baking powder

1 teaspoon salt

12 tablespoons (1½ sticks) unsalted butter, softened and cut into 12 pieces

Makes about 18 cupcakes

Instructions:

1. Set the oven rack in the middle position. Preheat the oven to 350 degrees. Line muffin pans with cup liners.

2. Pour the milk, egg whites, and vanilla extract into a medium bowl and mix with a fork until blended.

Directions for Electric Mixer
3. Mix the cake flour, sugar, baking powder, and salt in the bowl of an electric mixer at the lowest speed. Add the butter pieces; continue beating at slow speed until the mixture resembles moist crumbs, with no powdery ingredients remaining, about 1 minute.

4. Add all but ½ cup of the milk mixture to the crumbs and beat at medium speed for 1 minute. Add the remaining ½ cup of the milk mixture and beat 30 seconds longer. Stop the mixer and scrape the sides of the bowl. Return the mixer to medium speed and beat about 20 seconds longer. Continue with Step 5 on the next page.

Directions for Hand Mix
3. Mix the cake flour, sugar, baking powder, and salt in a large bowl using a whisk or spoon. Add the butter pieces; cut the butter into the flour mixture, with a pastry cutter or two knives until the mixture resembles the texture of moist crumbs, with no powdery ingredients remaining.

4. Add all but ½ cup of the milk mixture to the crumbs and mix with a large spoon until the milk is incorporated, 3 to 4 minutes. Add the remaining ½ cup of the milk mixture and mix vigorously for 1 to 2 minutes, until the batter looks fluffy and shiny.

5. Pour the batter into muffin cups so that the cups are about 80% full. Bake the cupcakes for 17 to 20 minutes. Insert a toothpick into the center of a cupcake; if it comes out clean, it is done.

6. Transfer the muffin pans to wire cooling racks or away from the hot oven. Let them cool for 10 minutes. Place your cupcakes onto a rack or a plate to continue to cool. Be sure to cool the cupcakes completely before frosting, about 1 hour.

Pastel Cakes

If you want your vanilla cake to be pink or blue instead of white, put a drop of red or blue food coloring into the vanilla cake batter just before you pour it into the bake cups. You can do this with any color food coloring . . . some like orange, purple, green, or yellow.

Cool It

After the cupcakes have baked, you can put them in the refrigerator to speed up the cooling process.

vanilla buttercream frosting

Creamy, dreamy, melts in your mouth

You need:

½ **pound (2 sticks)**
   unsalted butter,
   softened

1 pound (4 cups)
   confectioners' sugar

1 tablespoon pure vanilla
   extract

2 tablespoons heavy
   cream (or milk)

Pinch of salt

Instructions:

Directions for Electric Mixer
Beat the butter, confectioners' sugar, vanilla extract, heavy cream (or milk), and salt in the bowl of an electric mixer at low speed until the sugar is moistened. Increase the speed to medium and beat, stopping twice to scrape down the bowl, until creamy and fluffy, about 1½ minutes.

Directions for Hand Mix
Place the butter, vanilla extract, heavy cream (or milk), and salt in a large bowl. Carefully sift the sugar into the bowl. Beat with a large spoon until the frosting is smooth and fluffy, 6 to 8 minutes.

chocolate buttercream frosting
Follow the recipe for Vanilla Buttercream Frosting above but add ¾ cup unsweetened cocoa powder and another 2 tablespoons heavy cream or milk.

a cupcake decorating birthday party at home

What could be a more fun on your birthday than having your buddies over to decorate cupcakes?

And with "cupcaking," everyone gets to eat his or her yummy creations. Try it for your next party; everyone will love it. Here's how:

Before you send the invitations:
- Think of a party theme you like and include it in your cupcake decorating designs.
- When you write the invitations, say it's a "cupcaking" party! This will get your buddies excited. Also tell them to bring an apron or an old shirt because frosting can get messy.

The day before the party:
- Make some photocopies of the cupcake designs in this book that you'll want to do during your party.
- At your supermarket, buy the candies and sprinkles listed in this book that you'll need.
- Bake or buy your cupcakes. Be sure to have two or three cupcakes for each person.
- Make or buy vanilla and chocolate frostings. Put the chocolate frosting in a bowl, cover it, and put it in the refrigerator. Dump gobs of the vanilla frosting in other bowls, stir drops of different food colorings into each, to make pink, yellow, blue, green, and orange frostings. Cover these bowls and put them in the refrigerator as well.

The day of the party:
- Prepare your activity area. Pour the candies and sprinkles into bowls. Place all of the unfrosted cupcakes and the bowls of frosting on the activity table too. Also put out plastic knives, decorating tools, and the photocopies of cupcakes from this book.

At the party:
- Show your buddies how to get started: Spread the frosting!

Start Cupcaking

Lay out all of your candies and frostings in front of you. This way, all of your decorations will be close by and you can see all of them.

Have fun, and certainly don't worry if your cupcake looks different from the photos in the book. Remember, you're an artist with your own vision—and you can't make a mistake.

Here we go!

Level of Difficulty

One thing to remember: Some of these designs could take a while to create, others will probably not take long. Look at the symbols below so you'll know what's what.

Fairly simple

A few steps but not too many

Kind of complicated

cover me in sprinkles

Sprinkles dazzle and delight on top of little cakes—multicolored or solid, you pick.

You need:

Cupcakes

Colored, chocolate, or vanilla frosting— see page 24 for recipes

Sprinkles

Spoon

Knife

Small bowl

Instructions:

1. Frost the cupcake with any frosting;
(a) Drop a spoonful in the center of a cupcake;
(b) Use a knife to spread the frosting to the edges of the cupcake.

2. Pour the sprinkles into a small bowl.

3. Dip the cupcake into the bowl and rotate to cover all of the frosting with the sprinkles.

lots of polka dots

Pink . . . blue . . . yellow . . . green . . . orange—
any color is splendid atop a cupcake.
You can create a pattern with them or not.

You need:

Cupcakes

**Colored, chocolate, or
vanilla frosting—
see page 24 for recipes**

**Lots of candy dots
or brightly colored
disk-shaped candies
or tiny fruit-flavored
jelly candies**

Spoon

Knife

Plate

Paper Towels

Instructions:

1. Frost the cupcake with any frosting;
(a) Drop a spoonful in the center of a cupcake;
(b) Use a knife to spread the frosting to the edges of the cupcake.

2. Take the candy dots and place them on the cupcake in a pattern
or wherever you like.

my shining star

Stars shine, shimmer, and sparkle in the night sky and they twinkle on our treats.

You need:

Cupcakes

Colored, chocolate, or vanilla frosting—see page 24 for recipes

Colored sprinkles or sugar

Spoon

Knife

Star cookie cutter

Hint:

Repeat these instructions with a variety of colored sugars or sprinkles and frostings to create a slew of sassy stars.

Instructions:

1. Frost the cupcake with any frosting;
(a) Drop a spoonful in the center of cupcake.
(b) Use a knife to spread the frosting to edges of the cupcake.

2. Place the star cookie cutter on the top of the frosted cupcake.

3. Sprinkle the sprinkles inside the cookie cutter.

4. Carefully remove the cookie cutter from the cupcake to reveal a star shape on your cupcake.

light me up

Chanukah is a celebration of light. No doubt, this petite morsel will glimmer and glow on your holiday table.

You need:

Cupcakes

**Colored frosting—
  see page 24 for recipe**

**Blue, yellow, and red
  decorating gel**

Sprinkles

Spoon

Knife

Hint:

You can use decorating gel to draw any shape or thing your heart desires. It's really fun.

Instructions:

1. Frost the cupcake with any colored frosting;
(a) Drop a spoonful in the center of a cupcake;
(b) Use a knife to spread the frosting to the edges of the cupcake.

2. With blue decorating gel, draw a menorah on the frosted cupcake.

3. With yellow and red decorating gel, add candles and flames atop each branch of the menorah.

4. Sprinkle some sprinkles on the cupcake.

cherry on top

A cherry on top is the perfect crown
for a cute cupcake.

You need:

Cupcakes

**Vanilla frosting—see
page 24 for recipe**

Sour cherry candy

Black licorice string

Red decorating gel

Spoon

Knife

Instructions:

1. Frost the cupcake with vanilla frosting;
(a) Drop a spoonful in the center of a cupcake;
(b) Use a knife to spread the frosting to the edges of the cupcake.

2. Place the sour cherry candy into the center of the cupcake.

3. Carefully cut a small piece of black licorice string.

4. Place a small dot of red decorating gel on the top of the sour cherry.

5. Place the small piece of black licorice onto the top of the red decorating gel.

love you so much

Valentine's Day or any day is the right day to decorate your delights with heart shapes. You can savor your sweets with the sweetness of love.

You need:

Cupcakes

Colored, chocolate, or vanilla frosting— see page 24 for recipes

Heart-shaped cookie cutter

Colored sugar or sprinkles

Decorating gel

Spoon

Knife

Hint:

Try this with any cookie cutter shape you like or have at home. There are so many possibilities.

Instructions:

1. Frost the cupcake with any frosting;
(a) Drop a spoonful in the center of a cupcake;
(b) Use a knife to spread the frosting to the edges of the cupcake.

2. Place the cookie cutter on the top of the frosted cupcake.

3. Sprinkle colored sugar or sprinkles inside the cookie cutter.

4. Carefully remove the cookie cutter from the cupcake to reveal a heart shape on your cupcake.

wow! balloons!

What's a party without some balloons?
Here is a colorful bunch that you can chomp down on.

You need:

Cupcakes

**Colored frosting—
see page 24 for
recipe**

**Black and red licorice
string**

Fruit gem candy

Spoon

Knife

Scissors

Instructions:

1. Frost the cupcake with colored frosting;
(a) Drop a spoonful in the center of a cupcake;
(b) Use a knife to spread the frosting to the edges of the cupcake.

2. Cut pieces of black and red licorice string.

3. Place the fruit gems near the top of the cupcake.

4. Place the licorice string from the fruit gems to the bottom of the cupcake.

apple of my eye

A gift for the sunshine of your life or the apple of your eye

You need:

Cupcakes

Red frosting—see page 24 for recipe

Chocolate-covered mint stick candy

Green apple strip candy

Spoon

Knife

Hint:

You can repeat these instructions with lemon-colored frosting or orange-colored frosting to make a cupcake that looks like a lemon or an orange fruit.

Instructions:

1. Frost the cupcake with red frosting;
(a) Drop a spoonful in the center of the cupcake;
(b) Use a knife to spread the frosting to the edges of the cupcake.

2. Place the chocolate-covered mint stick into the center of the cupcake.

3. Carefully cut with scissors a leaf shape out of the green apple strip candy.

4. Place the strip candy into the center of cupcake.

stars and stripes

Hey, what has 50 stars and 13 red and white stripes on a stick? It's the American flag! Here's one to take a bite into.

You need:

Cupcakes

Vanilla frosting—
see page 24 for
recipe

Blue-colored
sugar decoration

Red licorice string

Spoon

Knife

Paper

Scissors

Instructions:

1. Frost the cupcake with vanilla frosting;
(a) Drop a spoonful in the center of a cupcake;
(b) Use a knife to spread the frosting to the edges of the cupcake.

2. Hold a piece of paper on top of the left upper corner of the cupcake. Sprinkle blue-colored sugar decoration over the left upper corner of the cupcake.

3. Cut with scissors seven short and medium-length pieces of licorice string. Place the licorice string on the cupcake to create stripes.

4. Insert a licorice string into the top of the cupcake to look like the flag's stick.

spider creep

Creepy spiders crawl atop cupcakes during Halloween. But these crawlers won't bite; they are treats to be treasured.

You need:

Cupcakes

**Orange frosting—
see page 24 for
recipe**

1 black candy dot

Black decorating gel

Spoon

Instructions:

1. Frost the cupcake with the orange frosting;
(a) Drop a spoonful in the center of a cupcake;
(b) Use a knife to spread the frosting to the edges of the cupcake.

2. Cut the black candy dot with scissors. Place a black dot near the top of the cupcake.

3. Use the black decorating gel to draw the spiders' spindly legs.

butterfly beauty

Ever look at the colors of a butterfly? Here's one that's pink and yellow, but other colors would be delightful too.

You need:

Cupcakes

Green frosting—see page 24 for recipe

Black licorice string

2 candy slices, one yellow and one pink

2 fruit-shaped candies

1 tiny jelly candy

Spoon

Knife

Scissors

Hint:

Try this with different colored candies—you can't go wrong.

Instructions:

1. Frost the cupcake with the green frosting;
(a) Drop a spoonful in the center of a cupcake;
(b) Use a knife to spread the frosting to the edges of the cupcake.

2. Cut the yellow and pink slices in half with scissors. Cut two short pieces of black licorice string.

3. Place the yellow slices in the center of the cupcake to form the butterfly's lower wings.

4. Place the jelly candy and the fruit-shaped candies between the wings to form the butterfly's body. Place pink slices to the sides of them to make the other set of wings. Place the black licorice on top of the body as antennae.

slithering snake

Some snakes are dangerous, but most are simply harmless. This one here on a bed of cookie crumbs is completely edible and quite a tasty treat.

You need:

Cupcakes

Chocolate or vanilla frosting—see page 24 for recipes

2 small chocolate cookies

2 gummy worms

Black decorating gel

Spoon

Knife

Plastic kitchen bag

Toothpick

Instructions:

1. Frost the cupcake with the chocolate or vanilla frosting;
(a) Drop a spoonful in the center of a cupcake;
(b) Use a knife to spread the frosting to the edges of the cupcake.

2. Place the chocolate cookies in a plastic kitchen bag. Crush the cookie bag in your hands, making sure some pieces are small crumbs and others are larger bits. Use the cookie crumbs to coat the frosted cupcake.

3. Arrange the gummy worms on top of the cookie crumbs. Press them into the cupcake or frosting so they look like they're crawling out of the ground.

4. Add the eyes with black decorating gel.

swimming fishes

A group of fish together is called a school of fish. This is a school of tiny, chewy, fruity fishies.

You need:

Cupcakes

Blue frosting–
    see page 24 for recipe

Blue, red, or yellow
    decorating gel

5 mini Swedish fish

Spoon

Knife

Instructions:

1. Frost the cupcake with the blue frosting:
(a) Drop a spoonful in the center of a cupcake;
(b) Use a knife to spread the frosting to the edges of the cupcake.

2. Squeeze some of the decorating gel onto the Swedish fish to create eyes.

3. Add the Swedish fish to the cupcake. They can swim around the cupcake any way you like.

darling daisies

What's prettier than a freshly picked daisy?
You can't beat four or five of 'em together in a bouquet.

You need:

Cupcakes

Yellow frosting–
    see page 24 for recipe

6 mini marshmallows

1 chocolate candy

2 sugary gel candies
    (optional)

Spoon

Knife

Scissors

Instructions:

1. Frost the cupcake with the yellow frosting:
(a) Drop a spoonful in the center of a cupcake;
(b) Use a knife to spread the frosting to the edges of the cupcake.

2. Cut the mini marshmallows in half with scissors.

3. Pinch the mini marshmallow half edges with your fingers to make a petal shape.

4. Place the chocolate candy on the cupcake to be the center of the flower.

5. Place the marshmallow petals around the chocolate candy in a circle.

6. If you like, you can cut the sugary gel candies to form a leaf and stem shape and place them on the cupcake below the daisy.

candy snowman

When it's very cold outside, nothing is more fun than making a candy snowman inside.

You need:

Cupcakes

**Blue frosting–
    see page 24 for
    recipe**

1 mini marshmallow

Black licorice string

1 small red candy

Coconut flakes

**2 regular-size
    marshmallows**

2 licorice candies

Spoon

Knife

Scissors

Instructions:

1. Frost the cupcake with the blue frosting:
(a) Drop a spoonful in the center of a cupcake;
(b) Use a knife to spread the frosting to the edges of the cupcake.

2. Place a mini marshmallow at the top of the cupcake as the snowman's head.

3. Cut two small pieces of black licorice string with scissors and place them on the marshmallow to make the eyes.

4. Place a red candy in the center of the marshmallow to be the nose.

5. Place the two regular-sized marshmallows below the mini marshmallow to be the snowman's body.

6. Insert the licorice candies on the sides of the middle marshmallow to make arms.

7. Sprinkle coconut flakes all over the snowman.

moonlight kitty

Ever seen a little kitty out on a moonlit night?

You need:

Cupcakes

Chocolate or vanilla frosting—see page 24 for recipe

Fruit gem candy

1 red candy dot

Blue sugar sprinkles

Black decorating gel

Red decorating gel

1 banana-shaped candy

Spoon

Knife

Scissors

Small bowl

Instructions:

1. Frost the cupcake with the chocolate or vanilla frosting:
(a) Drop a spoonful in the center of the cupcake.
(b) Use a knife to spread the frosting to edges of cupcake.

2. Cut the fruit gem candy into 3 little triangular pieces using scissors.

3. Cut the red candy dot in half.

4. Pour the blue sugar sprinkles into the small bowl.

5. Dip the cupcake into the bowl and rotate the cupcake to cover the frosting with the sprinkles.

6. Place the 2 halves of the red dot on the cupcake.

7. Add 2 pieces of fruit gem candy above the dot halves as ears.

8. Add the third piece of fruit gem candy at the side of the bottom red dot as the tail.

9. With the black decorating icing, make 2 dots for eyes and two dots for paws.

10. Place the banana-shaped candy on the cupcake as the moon.

birdy birdy birdy

Chirp. Chirp. Yum. Yum.

You need:

Cupcakes

**Vanilla frosting—
    see page 24 for recipe**

1 green candy dot

**1 yellow sugary
    gel candy**

**1 green sugary gel
    c andy**

1 red sugary gel candy

Red licorice string

Red decorating gel

Spoon

Knife

Scissors

Instructions:

1. Frost the cupcake with the vanilla frosting:
(a) Drop a spoonful in the center of a cupcake.
(b) Use a knife to spread the frosting to the edges of the cupcake.

2. Cut the yellow sugary gel candy in half.

3. Cut the orange sugary gel candy into a small triangle for the beak, and a red one into two triangles.

4. Cut two short pieces of licorice, which will be the legs.

5. Place the yellow sugary gel candy in the center of the cupcake. To the side of it, place a piece of red candy to be the bird's head.

6. Add the orange candy beak.

7. Put the licorice legs at the bottom of the birdy's body, and the red candy triangle as the tail.

8. Make a tiny eye on the bird's head with a drop of decorating gel.

crab claws

Crabs have large and powerful claws
and many little legs. Try these—they're mighty tasty.

You need:

Cupcakes

**White frosting–
  see page 24 for recipe**

**3 mini orange sugary
  gel candies**

Red licorice string

Blue decorating gel

Spoon

Knife

Scissors

Instructions:

1. Frost the cupcake with the blue frosting:
(a) Drop a spoonful in the center of a cupcake;
(b) Use a knife to spread the frosting to the edges of the cupcake.

2. Cut the 3 orange sugary gel candies in half so each one makes 2 thin circles.

3. Cut both of the circles in half to make 4 half-circles.

4. Put 3 half-circles to the side. Cut the last half-circle into 2 squares and 4 long triangles.

5. Cut the red licorice string into 6 short pieces and 2 tiny pieces using scissors.

6. Place 1 of the half-circles in the center of the cupcake.

7. Add a square to both sides of the half-circle.

8. Add a long triangle to both sides of the square.

9. Place the half-circles on the cupcake to create a claw.

(continue with steps on next page)

10. Add the other 2 long triangles to complete the claw.

11. Add the 6 short red licorice string pieces underneath the center half-circle.

12. Add the 2 tiny pieces of sugary fruit candy to the top of the center half-circle.

13. Add 2 dots of the blue decorating gel on top of the tiny pieces of sugary fruit candy to make the crab's eyes.

cupcakes at school

"Cupcaking" at school is great fun for holiday parties or classroom birthday parties. Ask your teacher if your class can do it. You can show him or her this book. Once he or she says okay, you can announce it during class or pass out invitations to your classmates. Be sure to tell them to bring in an apron or an old shirt on decorating day.

A few days before the party:
• Pack up the following items in a bag to bring to school: cupcakes, frosting, candies, this book, and plastic knives.
• Gather the frostings, both vanilla and chocolate. Make a variety of colors of frostings from the vanilla and divide the frostings into separate plastic bowls so that everyone can frost with any of the colors.
• Collect the candy decorations you will need.
• Have enough plastic knives for everyone to work with.

The day before the party :
• Collect the cupcakes. Be sure you have enough for everyone in your class. It is always better to have extra goodies than not enough goodies.

At school:
• Keep all of your cupcakes and frostings in a refrigerator and take them out just before you start your "cupcaking."
• You may need to place newspaper down on the tables before you start. If so, do so.
• Now get started: Pass around the cupcakes, frostings, and candies.
• Show your classmates this book so that they can get inspired.
• Then go for it! Have a blast.
• After you are finished, be sure to clean up the room with all your buddies.

gumballs galore

Dot your cupcake with a rainbow of gumballs!
It looks pretty sweet. Yeah!

You need:

Cupcakes

Chocolate or vanilla frosting–see page 24 for recipe

Black and red decorating gel

Nonpareil sprinkles

Spoon

Knife

Instructions:

1. Frost the cupcake with the chocolate or vanilla frosting:
(a) Drop a spoonful in the center of a cupcake;
(b) Use a knife to spread the frosting to the edges of the cupcake.

2. With the red decorating gel, create the gumball machine shape.

3. Carefully sprinkle the nonpareil sprinkles into the gumball machine circle.

4. With the black decorating gel, add the "10¢."

bunny rabbit ears

What a yummy bunny to hop around with on your Easter holiday—sure to be the best sweet in your basket!

You need:

Cupcakes

Vanilla frosting—
    see page 24 for recipe

Licorice string

1 red heart-shaped
    candy

2 mini marshmallows

2 tiny fruit-flavored
    jelly candies

Spoon

Knife

Scissors

Instructions:

1. Frost the cupcake with the vanilla frosting:
(a) Drop a spoonful in the center of a cupcake;
(b) Use a knife to spread the frosting to the edges of the cupcake.

2. With scissors, cut 6 medium-size licorice strings, about 1½ inches long, and 2 longer licorice strings, about 4 inches long, and 2 small ones, about an inch long.

3. Use the fruit-flavored jelly candies as the bunny's eyes.

4. Put the red heart-shaped candy in the center of the cupcake to be the bunny's nose, and use the two small licorice strings to make a smiling mouth.

5. Place the 2 mini marshmallows inside the mouth shape.

6. Stick the 6 small-size licorice strings into the center of the cupcake as whiskers.

7. Place the 2 medium-sized licorice strings into the top of the cupcake in the shape of ears.

rainbow sunshine

Have you ever seen a rainbow? Well, they appear when the sun shines during a rainfall. They're simply supernatural!

You need:

Cupcakes

White frosting—see page 24 for recipe

Marzipan (Sweetened almond paste called marzipan can be purchased at any fine food market or gourmet shop. Ask your grocer.)

Red, orange, yellow, green, and blue food coloring

Spoon

Knife

Waxed paper

Instructions:

1. Frost the cupcake with the white frosting:
(a) Drop a spoonful in the center of a cupcake;
(b) Use a knife to spread the frosting to the edges of the cupcake.

2. Make 5 separate small balls of marzipan by rolling pieces of marzipan in your hand.

(continue with steps on next page)

3. Add 1 drop of the red food coloring to 1 of the balls of marzipan. To make orange—add 1 drop of red and 1 drop of yellow to 1 of the balls of marzipan. To make yellow—add 1 drop of yellow to another of the marzipan balls. To make green—add 1 drop of green to another of the marzipan balls. To make blue—add 1 drop of blue to another of the marzipan balls.

4. For each marzipan ball, fold the marzipan over and over until the entire ball of marzipan is an even shade of color.

5. Roll each ball out into a rope.

6. Line up the strings in the following order: red, orange, yellow, green, blue. Then make an arch with the strings.

7. Cover the 5 strings with waxed paper. Press your hand down on the marzipan to flatten the strings together.

8. Lift the waxed paper off the marzipan. Place the marzipan rainbow on top of your frosted cupcake.

fuzzy sheep

Sheep's fur can be puffy and fuzzy and fluffy.
Here's some fur that's also yummy.

You need:

Cupcakes

Pale blue or chocolate frosting—see page 24 for recipe

6 mini marshmallows

1 black sugary gel candy

Black licorice string

Spoon

Knife

Scissors

Instructions:

1. Frost the cupcake with the frosting:
(a) Drop a spoonful in the center of a cupcake;
(b) Use a knife to spread the frosting to the edges of the cupcake.

2. Cut the 6 mini marshmallows in half. Flatten each marshmallow half with your fingers.

3. Lay the mini marshmallows on the cupcake. Start by putting some in a half-circle, then overlap more to create an inner circle.

(continue with steps on next page)

4. Cut the black gel candy in half and then cut again to make a triangular shape. Add the triangle piece just above the mini marshmallow pieces to be the sheep's face.

5. Cut the other half of the gel candy into ear-shaped pieces. Place the ear-shaped pieces to the sides of the triangular piece.

6. Cut 4 short pieces of black licorice string with scissors. Place the black licorice string pieces beneath the mini marshmallows.

sweetiepie pumpkin

Gobble. Gobble. Treasure your Thanksgiving Day treats with tiny little mini pumpkins.

You need:

Cupcakes

White frosting—
   see page 24 for recipe

Marzipan (Sweetened almond paste called marzipan can be purchased at any fine food market or gourmet shop. Ask your grocer.)

Red and orange food coloring

1 green licorice candy

Orange sugar glitter

Spoon

Knife

Scissors

Instructions:

1. Frost the cupcake with the white frosting:
(a) Drop a spoonful in the center of a cupcake.
(b) Use a knife to spread the frosting to the edges of the cupcake.

2. Make a small ball of marzipan by rolling a piece of marzipan in your hand. Add 1 drop of red food coloring and 1 drop of yellow food coloring to the ball of marzipan.

3. Fold the marzipan over and over until the entire ball of marzipan is an even shade of orange.

(continue with steps on next page)

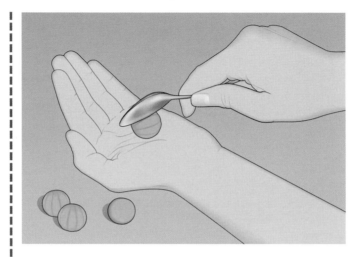

4. With your hands, flatten the top and bottom of the marzipan ball. With the side of a spoon make a little impression into the side of the marzipan ball. Make impressions on the side of the entire marzipan ball. Place the green licorice candy into the top of the marzipan ball.

5. Sprinkle the orange sugar glitter on the top of the cupcake. Place the orange marzipan pumpkin in the middle of the cupcake.

park picnic cupcakes

Are you going to the park for a picnic? Why not do some "cupcaking" there?
Pack your colorful apron and a big blanket, invite a few buddies, and you'll be sure to
have a great afternoon.

Your picnic party bag should include:
• A container of unfrosted cupcakes that you baked or bought at the store.
• You need frostings—either make some yummy vanilla and chocolate frosting or buy
some. Before you leave your house, be sure to color your vanilla frosting a few different
colors so that there is a good variety for you to play with. Place these in plastic containers.
• Collect your decoration candies, some plastic knives, paper napkins, and this book,
of course.
• A few other essentials are needed for a safe park event: sunscreen, jugs of water, and
proper clothes in case a breeze picks up.

Now off to the park:
• Head to a spot in the park that you like. This could be near a zoo or near a beautiful
garden.
• If there happens to be someone selling balloons in the park, you may want to ask your
parent or friend to purchase a few to decorate your picnic area.
• Lay out your blanket; arrange your cakes and decorating supplies; put on your apron;
open your book; and start "cupcaking." Don't be surprised if park passersby ask what you
are doing. Smile and tell them you are "cupcaking."

racing cars

Zooooooom! Ziiiiiiip! Whooshhhhh!
These speeding cars are whizzing down the racetrack.

You need:

Cupcakes

Gray frosting—
    see page 24 for recipe

2 Mexican hat-shaped
    jellies or 2 hard
    candies

4 tiny fruit-flavored
    jelly candies

Decorating gel

White tiny oval-shaped
    hard candies

Spoon

Knife

Scissors

Instructions:

1. Frost the cupcake with the gray frosting:
(a) Drop a spoonful in the center of a cupcake.
(b) Use a knife to spread the frosting to the edges of the cupcake.

2. Using scissors, cut off the edges of the Mexican hat-shaped jellies on two sides.

3. Cut the tiny fruit-flavored jelly candies in half with scissors.

4. With the decorating gel, make dots on the tiny jelly candy halves. Attach the halves to the Mexican hat-shaped candy (or hard candy)—the decorating gel works as glue.

5. Place the white tiny oval-shaped hard candies on the cupcake in a line down the middle.

6. Place the racing cars on the cupcake.

chew choo train

Over 200 years ago, which is a VERY long time ago, trains were invented. These trains helped people and materials to be moved to and from faraway places.

You need:

Cupcakes

Green frosting— see page 24 for recipe

2 striped layer candies

Black licorice string

8 chocolate chips

Spoon

Knife

Scissors

Instructions:

1. Frost the cupcake with green frosting:
(a) Drop a spoonful in the center of a cupcake;
(b) Use a knife to spread the frosting to the edges of the cupcake.

2. Cut a tiny piece of black licorice string with scissors.

3. Place the two striped layer candies on the cupcake.

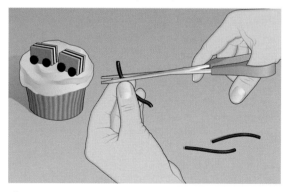

4. Place the chocolate chips at the base of each "boxcar" to be the wheels. Use a drop of frosting as glue if you need it to hold the wheels in place.

5. Place the small piece of black licorice string between the boxcars. Use a tiny dab of frosting to glue it if necessary.

christmas yum

Christmas dessert can be a handsome handmade chocolate tree on top of a cupcake.

Adult supervision is necessary.

You need:

Cupcakes

White or green frosting—see page 24 for recipe

2 ounces chocolate (We used semisweet chocolate here but you could use milk, white, or dark chocolate.)

8 to 10 circle sprinkles

Spoon

Knife

Pencil

Paper

Waxed paper

Plastic kitchen bag

Scissors

Plate

Instructions:

1. Frost the cupcake with the green frosting:
(a) Drop a spoonful in the center of a cupcake;
(b) Use a knife to spread the frosting to the edges of the cupcake.

2. Make an outline of a Christmas tree with a pencil and paper. Place waxed paper down on the counter on top of the Christmas tree drawing.

3. Ask your parent for help with melting chocolate either in a microwave or in a double boiler.

If you are using a microwave, place the chocolate in a microwavable dish. Microwave on high for 30 seconds. Stir the chocolate. If the chocolate is not fully melted, return the dish to the microwave and microwave again for 30 seconds on high.

If you use the double boiler method, pour water into a medium pot. Then place the chocolate in a small pot and place the small pot in the medium pot. Turn the stove to low heat. Continually stir the chocolate in the pot. When the chocolate is melted, turn the stove off.

(continue with steps on next page)

4. When the chocolate is melted, let cool for 1 minute. Then scoop the chocolate into a plastic kitchen bag. With scissors, snip a tiny hole in the corner of the bag. Trace the outline of the Christmas tree by slowly squeezing the chocolate out of the bag onto the waxed paper.

5. Fill in the outline of the Christmas tree by continuing to squeeze chocolate out of the bag. Place the circle sprinkles on the melted chocolate.

6. Put the waxed paper on a plate and place it in your refrigerator freezer so it can harden. When the Christmas tree has fully hardened, approximately 20 minutes in the freezer, place it on top of your cupcake.

Hint:

The chocolate Christmas tree may need support when placed on the cupcake—you can prop it up with a piece of candy or with a spoonful of frosting.

save the memories

Making art work at school is super duper fun. It's equally fun to show off your art-work when you get home. Your drawing or collage may get taped to the refrigerator door or hung on the wall in your room. The same can go for your edible art! But these pieces need to be recorded before you take a bite into them.

Take Photos:
• Ask a family member to take some of photos of you with your cupcake creations. Also, take a photo or two just of the cupcake. And lastly, have someone shoot a snap of you eating your sugary sweet. When you have the photograph in your hand, you can sign the photo with a Sharpie pen and pin the photo of your creations on your wall.

Create a List:
• When you have a bunch of pals over for a "cupcaking" event, ask a family member or a friend to make a record of the party. Start with the date and the name of the party, like *November 8, 2005–Elaine's Cupcake Birthday Party.* Then list each person's name and ask each of them which cupcake creation they made. Also ask them what they want to name their cupcake. After you have quizzed everyone, ask everyone to take a bite of his or her gooey creations. You can ask each buddy to describe how his or her cupcake tasted. Write that down too!

Send Letters:
• Make photocopies of each of your photos and send them to your buddies at the party. They will love to be reminded of their day at your "cupcaking" event. Be sure to include the date of the party, the title of their creation, and the few words they used to describe how their treat tasted. They will surely be excited to receive your letter.

bangs and braids

What's your hair look like? Got any bangs?
Ever wear braids?

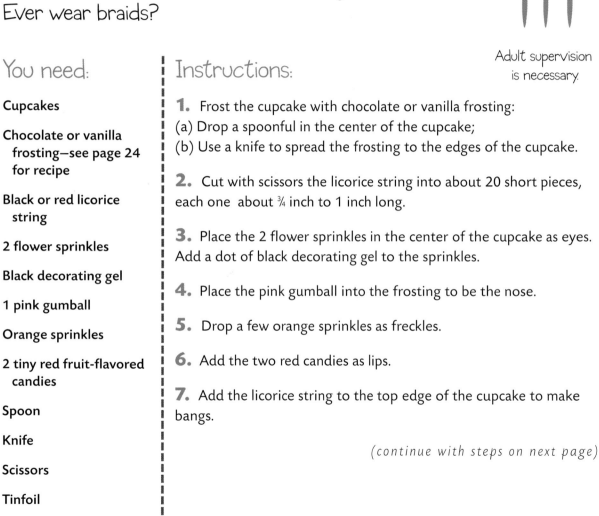

Adult supervision
is necessary.

You need:

Cupcakes

Chocolate or vanilla frosting—see page 24 for recipe

Black or red licorice string

2 flower sprinkles

Black decorating gel

1 pink gumball

Orange sprinkles

2 tiny red fruit-flavored candies

Spoon

Knife

Scissors

Tinfoil

Instructions:

1. Frost the cupcake with chocolate or vanilla frosting:
(a) Drop a spoonful in the center of the cupcake;
(b) Use a knife to spread the frosting to the edges of the cupcake.

2. Cut with scissors the licorice string into about 20 short pieces, each one about ¾ inch to 1 inch long.

3. Place the 2 flower sprinkles in the center of the cupcake as eyes. Add a dot of black decorating gel to the sprinkles.

4. Place the pink gumball into the frosting to be the nose.

5. Drop a few orange sprinkles as freckles.

6. Add the two red candies as lips.

7. Add the licorice string to the top edge of the cupcake to make bangs.

(continue with steps on next page)

8. Cut some more licorice string into 6 equal pieces about 7 inches long. In a preheated 300-degree F oven, place the licorice string on tinfoil in a baking pan and leave it for 15 minutes, or until easily bendable. Remove from oven. Let the hot licorice cool about 2 minutes, or until you can comfortably hold it.

9. Take 3 licorice pieces and braid them together. Take the other 3 pieces and braid them also.

10. Place braids on the sides of the cupcake.

Can't think of anything better than playing

with color and candy?

Have a blast—everything you make

will most certainly be great.

Index
